Aberdeen

in old picture postcards

by
Janey and John Clark

European Library – Zaltbommel/Netherlands

GB ISBN 90 288 4852 5 / CIP

INTRODUCTION

'Aberdeen is the one haunting and exasperatingly lovable city in Scotland,' according to Lewis Grassic Gibbon. It is a City which collects nicknames – The Silver City, The Granite City, Offshore Capital of Europe and Scotland's North Sea Gateway and distinctions such as City of Three Cathedrals, Gateway to the Grampians, the World's Busiest Helicopter Port and several times winner of the 'Britain in Bloom' competition.

Aberdeen lies between the Rivers Dee and Don on Scotland's north-east coast. Miles of fine sandy beaches have long been used for recreation. The Grampian mountains keep rainfall to moderate levels which, together with long hours of summer sunshine, assist this to be a fine agricultural area. Aberdeen's prosperity has been based on agriculture, fishing, quarrying and a wide range of service industries.

There is evidence of settlements in the area for over 2,000 years. Aberdeen entered documented history in the twelfth century with the City's oldest charter confirming established privileges. Originally the City was based around the Green but growing prosperity led to a shift to the Castlegate. Robert the Bruce supported the City's growth by granting additional rights and privileges. Aberdeen consolidated its position as Scotland's third City over the following centuries.

The eighteenth century saw many changes; the first granite quarry opened in 1730, important new buildings included Robert Gordon's College and the first Infirmary, new institutions included the first coffee houses and banks and the establishment of the Aberdeen Journal. At the end of the century the City decided to expand leading to the construction of Union Street. In 1801, 27,000 people lived in 30 streets and by 1901, 153,000 people resided in 500 streets.

The nineteenth century saw many innovations but Aberdeen survived the Victorian boom as well as any city. The railway arrived in 1850, after gas lighting and the Penny Post but before the first proper sewage system, trams, electricity and telephones. This was the period when Aberdeen truly became the Granite City under the supervision of several architects foremost of whom were John Smith and

Archibald Simpson. In 1891 the separate authorities of Aberdeen, Old Aberdeen and Woodside amalgamated.

The twentieth century has seen yet more development. Retailing altered after F.W. Woolworth's opened the city's first multiple store in 1914. From 1912 the cinema was a mainstay of entertainment until television arrived in 1954. The changes from about 1970 were even more dramatic. Rubislaw Quarries closed the year after oil was discovered offshore and Aberdeen became an oil port. The New Market was demolished and St. Nicholas House built. People from all over the world have settled in and around Aberdeen. Over the centuries Aberdeen has seen many changes, a little of which may be seen in postcards from our collection, but it remains one of the country's finest cities.

We have to thank many people for help in preparing this modest volume including: City of Aberdeen Central Library, Art Gallery and Museum, Scottish Fisheries Museum, Aberdeen Harbour Board, Robert Gordon's College, British Sailor's Society, Bucksburn Church of Scotland, National Railway Museum, N.A.A.F.I., Harlaw Academy, Hazlehead & Aberdeen Academy F.P. Club, Scottish Red Cross and C. Bruce Miller as well as lots of friends and relations. We would stress that any mistakes are entirely our own.

The postcards were published by firms of all sizes. Aberdeen publishers include G.W. Wilson, McMillan, T. Lamb, James Donald, Strachan, George Dickie, W.L. Dunn, M. Monro, Rattray, C. Heimrich, Catto & Watt, A & R Milne and from Bucksburn, A.J. Bruce and John Gray. Valentines of Dundee are well represented. The cards were printed all over Scotland as well as England, France and Germany.

The book is laid out from Union Street and moves to Old Aberdeen, the Harbour and then the west of the City. Cards illustrate local occupations and businesses followed by buildings and parks. A few cards show suburban views and we conclude with the beach and a few miscellaneous cards.

Janey Macgregor was born in Aberdeen. She and her husband John Clark live in Portishead near Bristol and remain regular visitors to Aberdeen.

1. *Salvation Army Citadel, Castle Street.* Castle Street, with the Salvation Army Citadel looming over the market area, is a superb terminal to Union Street. The Citadel, built in 1893, owes a clear debt to Balmoral Castle. The statue to the right is of George, fifth and last Duke of Gordon (1770-1836). It was sculpted in 1842 and remained here until 1952 when it was removed to Golden Square. The Duke raised the Corps which is now known as the Second Battalion of the Gordon Highlanders. In Aberdeen, unlike many cities, the statues of soldiers are outnumbered by statues of poets and sovereigns.

2. *Castle Street, the Athenaeum Restaurant.* The Athenaeum was designed as a newsroom by Archibald Simpson but for over one hundred years it was a restaurant. Gutted by fire in 1973 and restored five years later, it was rebuilt as offices without a public restaurant. The vehicles parked in neat rows with notice boards leaning against their radiators are char-à-bancs offering trips and tours. Their 'toast rack' shape can be easily seen in an aerial view of Union Street.

3. *Timmer Market.* The Timmer Market is held annually in Castle Street on the last Wednesday in August. It moved to Justice Street Car Park in 1935 but has now returned to Castle Street. It specialised in wooden goods including toys, spurtles, bassies, washtubs and tattie chappers. A card bears the following lines: *This market day we ill could spare,/ For though o'timmer unco bare,/ There's routh o'smachrie, wealth o'toys,/ For merry-hearted girls and boys./ And here they come from Brig o'Dee,/ And Fittie Square doon by the sea,/ From sleepy Aulton, brisk Woodside,/ And Rubislaw, where the gentry bide,/ From fair Rosemount and Torry braes,/ They come wi' hale and clooted claes,/ From Bawbie Law's and Split the Win',/ Wi' hurrying feet and deevin' din,/ They rush in croods to spend and play,/ This joyous Timmer Market Day,/ Time was, my friend, your heart and mine/ Were blithe as theirs in Auld Lang Syne!*

4. *Mercat Cross*. There are plenty of cards clearly showing the Mercat Cross but we selected this snow scene from 1908. Originally built in 1686 by John Montgomery, a master mason of Old Rayne, it was restored in 1820. Above the six arches are portraits of ten Stuart monarchs. There is a white marble unicorn on top of the central column. Without doubt it is the finest Mercat Cross in Scotland.

5. *Union Bridge.* Union Bridge has been altered since its completion in 1805 and this view is after 1914 with King Edward's statue in place. The signal gantry in the Den Burn Valley is absent from earlier pictures and has since given way to modern equipment. The iron lions, known as 'Kelly's cats', were saved during the 1965 rebuilding and are captive in the Duthie Park.

6. *Union Bridge looking west.* This is a G.W. Wilson card published by McMillan Ltd., Aberdeen, looking west some time before 1908. The stone parapet flanks the roadway with setts still in place. The Northern Assurance Building on the corner (now the Commercial Union Insurance) is graced by a wealth of architectural ornamentation. It is nicknamed 'The Monkey House' – a favourite meeting place for courting couples. A branch of Lloyds Bank was opened immediately to the right in 1979, replacing the building long occupied by the Caledonian Insurance Company.

7. *Union Terrace.* Union Terrace, with Prince Albert's statue in its original site, appears on this card. It is a bronze made in 1863 by Baron Carlo Marochetti showing the Prince in the uniform of a Field Marshal with the Robe of the Thistle over it. The unveiling of the statue was the first public function performed by Queen Victoria in her widowhood. The terrace has right-angled corners which were replaced by curves when the statue of Prince Albert was moved to make way for that of his son, King Edward VII, in 1914.

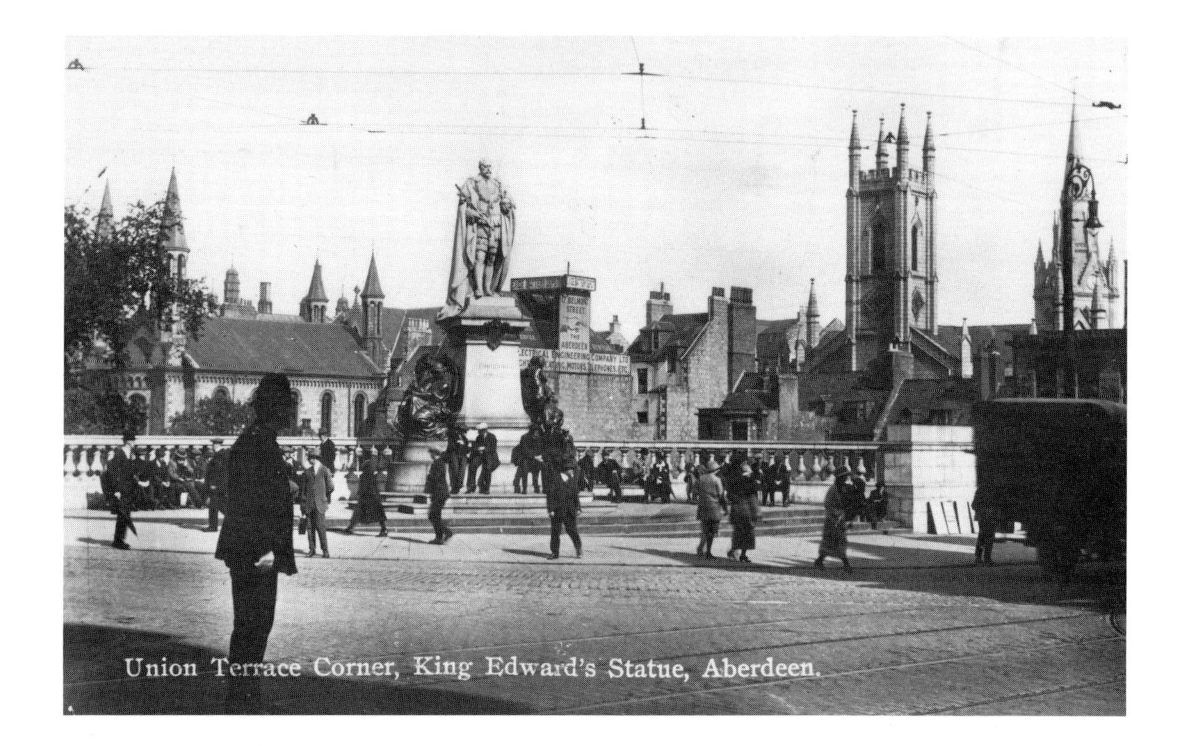

8. *King Edward's Statue.* King Edward VII is the last monarch to have given his name to a period of history. This monument by Alfred Drury, in granite and bronze, was unveiled on 31 October 1914, his father's statue having been moved further along Union Terrace. In the advertisement in the background the Aberdeen Electrical Engineering Company Ltd., 17 Belmont Street, offers Exide Batteries, lighting, heating, motors and telephones. They provided 'complete electric light systems where power may be derived from either turbine, steam, gas or oil engines'.

9. *Burns Statue.* A bronze by Henry Bainsmith erected in 1892 commemorates Scotland's greatest poet. Burns has a few points in common with Byron – both died in their thirties leaving a reputation for unorthodox views, having too many lady friends and an international reputation as poets. Byron wrote of Burns: 'What an antithetical mind! – tenderness, roughness-delicacy, coarseness-sentiment, sensuality-soaring and grovelling, dirt and diety – all mixed up in that one compound of 'inspired clay'. Burns' family lived near Aberdeen in his grandparents' day and he visited the city in 1787, calling Aberdeen 'a lazy town'.

Palace Hotel, Aberdeen

10. *Palace Hotel.* The Palace Hotel stood on the corner of Union Bridge. It was designed by James Matthews in 1873 as a drapery store but became a hotel in the ownership of the Great North of Scotland Co. in 1891. A lift gave easy access from the entrance opposite the Joint Railway Station. In 1914 a single room cost from four shillings and six pence, a double room from seven shillings and six pence, breakfast and lunch three shillings each and dinner five shillings. The hotel was destroyed by fire in 1941 and the site is now occupied by C & A Modes.

11. *His Majesty's Theatre.* This card was posted in 1917 only three years after Prince Albert's statue was moved to this spot. Trees have blocked this view of His Majesty's Theatre in recent years. The theatre was built in 1906 to a design by a Londoner, Frank Matcham and provides a 74 feet by 56 feet stage. It opened with a spectacular production of 'Little Red Riding Hood' including a ballet in falling snow. A souvenir of opening night said: 'We have come a period when the increasing strain of our daily business lives demands greater relaxations: when the rational ideal bids us cultivate everything that art, fancy, humour and instruction can do to sweeten the daily round.' Since then patrons of the 2,300 dark crimson seats have been entertained by everything from melodrama to Tahitian dancers.

12. *Central Library*. The Free South Church, designed by Marshall Mackenzie in 1892, is now St. Mark's Church. This handsome kirk is the centre-piece of the famous trio of buildings known as 'Education, Salvation and Damnation'. The Public Library is in its original 1891 condition. The extension to the left, which appears on another card of Rosemount Viaduct, has spoilt the symmetry of the building. At this time the Library was open from 9 am until 10 pm six days a week. There is a space to the right of the church where the theatre will be erected in 1904-1906.

13. *Wallace Statue.* The Liberator was modelled by Grant Stevenson in bronze one hundred years ago. He is shown declaring 'We will set Scotland free!'. It is the finest statue of him anywhere. One wonders what he would make of politics today. When the card was posted in 1916 thousands of Scottish soldiers were dying alongside English soldiers fighting for the freedom of Belgium. He would probably have approved, given his fierce hatred of foreign occupation and oppression.

14. *Rosemount Viaduct.* Rosemount Viaduct was constructed in stages from 1883. This card, printed before 1914, shows the Central Library to the right and on the left Nos 1-27 Rosemount Viaduct. The block has been called Aberdeen's most urban tenement and it is certainly elegant. Aberdeen's tenements, although built with only one or two rooms to each dwelling, were of a higher standard than those of other Scottish cities. The modest scale of each development together with small architectural flourishes make them quite distinctive. New lamp posts are about the only change to this scene.

15. *Cowdray Hall.* The Cowdray Hall sits on the junction of Schoolhill and Blackfriars Street, adjacent to the Art Gallery. It was built in 1925 with a suitably sombre War Memorial. The Triple Kirks on the opposite corner are no longer used for worship. The east part has become Simpson's restaurant, named after the famous architect. In the left foreground is the entrance to Schoolhill Station, with its platform stretching to the right lined with advertisements. This was part of Aberdeen's suburban system (Great North of Scotland Railway originally but by this date, L.N.E.R.). The station closed on 5 April 1937.

16. *Market Hall.* The Market Hall stood at the upper end of Market Street. Over 100 yards long it was originally erected in 1840-1842 at a cost of £28,000. It was restored after a fire in 1882. It was dismantled in 1971 in spite of considerable local outcry. The British Home Stores replacement includes a modestly sized market. The card was printed about 1905 in Saxony for J.R. Russell, Edinburgh.

17. *The Green.* The Green is believed to be the ancient centre of Aberdeen. The Green gets over forty references in 'City by the Grey North Sea', three times as many as any other street, which reflects its importance over the years. These turn-of-the-century furniture dealers appear to be selling secondhand goods, a quite different business to the new furniture shops of Union Street. The last of the Green's medieval houses, Andrew Aedie's lodging (1633), seen here as John Buchan's bakery, was demolished in 1914.

18. *Butter and Egg Market, The Green.* This card, postally used in 1913, gives a view of the Green Well popularly called the 'Mannie in the Green' or the 'Mannie Well'. The well was originally set up by William Lindsay in 1708 on Castlegate but remained in the Green from 1852 until 1958. It was rebuilt on Castlegate in 1972. Butter and eggs, like fish, are part of the great trading tradition of this spot.

19. *St. Nicholas Street.* 'Raggie' Morrison's store has been long remembered for the wide variety of goods it sold. At the corner of St. Nicholas Street H. Samuel, the jewellers, made way for the Commercial Bank in the 1930's. This junction was known as 'The Queen' after Queen Victoria's bronze statue of 1893 which was, appropriately, moved to Queen's Cross in 1964. St. Nicholas Street sweeps into George Street in this view, now blocked by the St. Nicholas shopping centre development. The Woodside tram is the only mechanical vehicle in sight and a street-sweeper cleans up after the horses.

20. *Union Street.* Union Street on a busy day has a wide range of transport including trams, buses, motor cars, motor cycles and sidecars, and horse-drawn carts. Parked in front of the Athenaeum are char-à-bancs. The nearer tower is the Old Tolbooth.

21. *Union Street, from the air.* An aerial view of many of the buildings shown in detail elsewhere which is believed to date from 1938. The Market Hall is prominent to the left, Marischal College, Robert Gordon's College and Rosemount Viaduct to the right and St. Nicholas Kirk in the centre.

Table Set for King's Luncheon in Town Hall, Aberdeen, 27th September, 1906.

22. *Town Hall.* The Town Hall is set for a luncheon visit by King Edward VII on the day he opened the extension to Marischal College. It is located within the New Town House which is dominated externally by the 190 feet high clocktower. The City has Scotland's finest set of civic documents, dating back to 1398, preserved in the Charter Room. An extension built in 1971 houses the present Council Chamber.

23. *Troops in Union Street.* Troops, led by pipers, march past 393-399 Union Street. The building, now occupied by the Halifax Building Society, was built about 1830. About 1910 there were different businesses in each bay: P. Beveridge, linen manufacturer, on the corner; W. & J. Bowie, dyers and cleaners, in the centre and G. & W. Morgan, photographers, at No. 393. Alfred Edward, bookseller, at No. 395 is not clear in this view. There has been some small alterations to the windows of the building in Bon Accord Terrace.

24. *Union Street, Capitol Cinema.* Union Street is shown in the mid-thirties with the Capitol Cinema on the right. Opposite, Archibald McKellar's grocery shop is followed by a tobacconist and civil and military tailors. The Capitol Cinema opened in February 1933 with Joan Crawford starring in 'Letty Lynton'. The cinema set new standards in entertainment; facilities included a very complicated lighting system, a large stage for live shows and a 120 seat tea terrace. For many patrons the evening's highlight occurred when a spotlight illuminated the art-deco console of the first theatre organ in the north of Scotland. The organ made by John Compton of London cost about £2,500 to install. The same year you could buy a new Morris Oxford car for £285!

25. *Union Street, East and West Churches.* St. Nicholas Kirk is identified in this card as the East and West Churches. They sport a Victorian 'Gothic' tower joining the West Church of 1755 to the East Church of 1875-77. The former hides in its dark interior a fine oak pulpit and other points of interest. Following the Reformation the old kirk fell into disrepair and it was occupied by Cumberland's troops on their way to Culloden. The road in front of the colonade has long been used as a taxi-rank, at the date of this card by horse-drawn carriages and in later views by horseless carriages!

26. *Union Street, Open Tram.* No. 34 tram for Queens Cross waits opposite Market Street while passengers climb aboard. The driver watches the queue. By 1909, 40 out of the city's 69 trams had been covered, serving all the regular services. A large pram nearly masks the lady pushing it.

27. *Union Street, Music Hall.* 'As one walks along Union Street,' writes Mervyn Jones 'one has the impression of being in a capital of a small but not a poor or a humble nation; a capital with style and character, like Dublin or Amsterdam or Oslo.' This postcard supports this opinion as the Music Hall carries echoes of Dublin's Law Courts. In fact the grand Ionic Porch is the entrance to the Assembly Rooms, yet another Simpson design from 1820. The Music Hall itself was added in 1858 by James Matthews and backs onto Golden Square. For 150 years this delightful building has provided a refined social centre for Aberdonians.

28. *Union Street, Rose Street.* The Bridge of Dee tram advertising 'Vino is Minty' is passing Findlay's Dairy, Chivas Brothers and Dundee Equitable Boot Depot on the right. On the other side of the road, business signs can be seen in the names of David Wilson (a watchmaker), Walter Simpson (plumber) and J.J. Stewart (draper). C. Weir, a ladies' and children's hosier and glover, advertises on the corner of Chapel Street. The view is about 1910 and the ornament on the pediment of Simpson's does not appear in the Capitol Cinema card about twenty years later.

29. *King Street.* The corner of King Street and Castle Street has been called the Hinge of the City. The imposing building on the left was built as the North of Scotland Bank in 1842. It is now the Clydesdale Bank with the terracotta statue of Ceres (the Goddess of Plenty, also known as Demeter) still in place just below the roof. In the middle of the picture is the North Church which is twelve years older. Students of architecture will contrast its Ionic columns with the Corinthian style of the Clydesdale Bank. It was converted into an Arts Centre in the 1950's.

30. *Union Street, Horses.* The early years of the century finds a selection of horse-drawn vehicles in Union Street. They include a cart, a two-wheeled gig and several carriages including one with buttoned upholstery. The 'Roman classic style' building was the North of Scotland and Town and Country Bank.

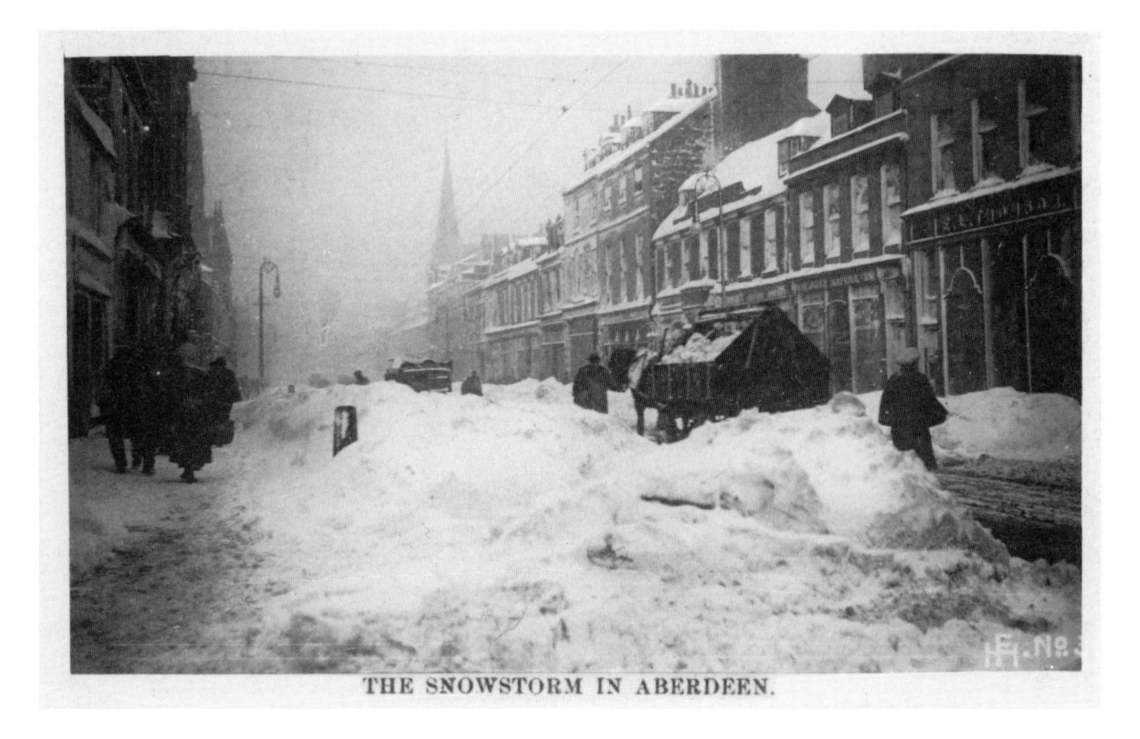

31. *Union Street, snow.* This card shows the same storm as the card of the Mercat Cross with a solitary horse-drawn cart attempting to clear the street.

32. *Union Street, closed tram.* A later view from the same spot as cards nos. 26 and 30. Posted in 1915 it illustrates the first covered trams, many of which were conversions of the original open top vehicles. The driver is still out in the fresh air and both ends of the top deck remain open. Hay & Lyall's shop on the right displays a very large 'By Appointment' sign. They sold clocks and works of art at 73 Union Street.

33. *Union Street, Commercial Bank.* The last classical building in Union Street was built in 1936 as the Commercial Bank of Scotland. It is today the Royal Bank of Scotland. It replaced H. Samuel and neighbouring shops shown on another card of St. Nicholas Street.

34. *Union Street, façade.* The façade of St. Nicholas's Churchyard appears in other photographs but wintry scenes are less common. It was built in 1829 and is considered to have been influenced by a similar structure at Hyde Park Corner, London. In the author's experience a snowfall like this would bring London's traffic to a standstill yet in 1913, when the card was posted, Aberdeen's traffic kept moving. There is snow on the men's caps but they have no overcoats. The card was sent to a Mr. J. Smith, quartermaster on S.S. City of Calcutta, who has just passed his Second Mates Certificate. It has never been easy to rise from Ordinary Seaman to become a Merchant Navy Officer so let us hope that Mr. Smith was not a casualty in the looming World War.

35. *Old Machar Cathedral, aerial view.* This postcard clearly illustrates that the St. Machar's we have today is only half of the original church. It has long been a place of worship and this St. Machar's was built between 1357 and 1522. It used granite boulders gathered from the fields long before the granite quarries opened. The remains of the transepts can be seen immediately east (right) of the building. The central spire fell in 1688 leaving the nave and smaller west towers. Bishop Dunbar was responsible for these towers, the old Greyfriars Church and for starting work on the Bridge of Dee. His tomb is in the ruined South Transept. The area is now one of Aberdeen's conservation areas.

36. *St. Machar's Nave.* This card shows the Nave looking west. The large organ was built in 1890 and was moved and rebuilt elsewhere in the Cathedral in 1929. It has three manuals controlling over 2,000 pipes. This fine instrument has often been used for broadcasts. The west window with 'Gothic Revival' tracery constructed in 1880 was replaced in 1953. The replacement was made possible by a legacy from Mrs. Florence Crombie of Parkhill House. The new stained glass window by William Wilson is very much more in keeping with the simple interior. The majestic wooden ceiling is still in place complete with the Pope's Coat of Arms but the bands around the pillars have been removed.

37. *Old Town Hall.* In 1891 Old Aberdeen, New Aberdeen and Woodside Burghs amalgamated into one political unit. Old Aberdeen's Town Hall is the city's finest Georgian building. When built in 1788 it included a Grammar and English school and today includes a public library and a masonic lodge in the old council chamber. Little has changed except for the street lights.

38. *High Street and King's College.* Until the 1950's one could look inland from the beach towards Old Aberdeen and only see the towers of St. Machar's and King's College Chapel. These are now swamped in a mass of modern development. King's College was founded by Bishop Elphinstone in 1494 and its handsome tower was originally built in 1515. Each subsequent century has seen additions to the College. It is now amalgamated with Marischal College to form the University of Aberdeen. For over two hundred years there were as many universities in Aberdeen as there were in the whole of England.

39. *King's College Chapel.* The College's greatest artistic treasure is the Chapel. It contains the only original set of choir stalls and choir screen in Scotland. It is believed that they were carved by an Aberdonian named John Fendour. No two carvings are identical and much use is made of thistles to decorate the panels. The Chapel, originally the Chapel of St. Mary in the Nativity, was built between 1500 and 1505, and is Gothic architecture of flamboyant style. A pulpit taken from the Cathedral dates from about 1545.

40. *College Bounds*. College Bounds is the last leg of the 'Spital Brae' from Aberdeen to Old Aberdeen. The Powis Towers were erected in 1834 as the east gate to College Bounds. The Coat of Arms of the Lairds of Powis decorates the structure.

41. *Harbour from the air.* This view shows the layout of the harbour for most of the century. The lock gates and swing bridge to the right have been removed to improve access. Sheerlegs used for handling heavy lifts until 1975 can be seen by the lock. Other points of interest are the floating dock, the large number of fishing craft on the left and what appears to be S.S. St. Sunniva. This vessel transported passengers, mail and general cargo to northern ports and the Shetlands.

42. *Aberdeen harbour.* Two coal boats are discharging at the head of the harbour. On the left is the steamer 'Thrift' built in 1904 for the Northern Co-operative Society Ltd. by Hall Russell & Co. The 500 ton ship survived torpedo attacks in the First World War and was sold in 1931 changing her name to 'Berryden'. She was finally broken up in 1953. Coal is being loaded into Great North of Scotland railway wagons. The coal was tipped into the holds on Tyneside and bagged up in Aberdeen – backbreaking, labour intensive work. Much of the coal was used by Aberdeen's steam trawlers. The last Aberdeen owned collier 'Ferryhill II' was sold in 1978. A few chartered vessels have discharged coal since but today coal usually arrives by rail.

43. *Harbour with trawlers.* A.941 was the steam trawler 'Pretoria' built by Hall Russell in 1900. A vessel of 61 tons she belonged in the 1920's to A.A. Davidson. Behind her is the 'Star of Britain' (A.239) which had been built by J. Duthie, Torry, in 1908 and was part of a fleet owned by Walker Steam Trawler Co. The three vertical lights shown by all fishing vessels are visible on her mast. Between the wars there were over 300 similar craft operating from Aberdeen. Steam trawlers continued in service until the 1960's when they were replaced by motor-vessels. Post-war craft burnt oil but these vessels were part of the great coal-fired fleet.

44. *Sailing craft.* These two dozen sailing fishing craft passing the breakwater light represents a small fraction of Aberdeen's fleet in the 1880's and 1890's. There is very little wind and AN.788 is using large oars to assist the sails. Work on such open craft, whether zulus, fifies or smacks, was usually cold and wet as well as heavy. The AN.126 was 'Tantallan Castle' owned in 1905 by James Craig. She had a keel of only 20 feet compared with the 100 feet of the steam trawlers. An example of a larger boat, the fifie 'Reaper' is maintained by the Scottish Fisheries Museum, Anstruther, Fife.

45. *Herring gutters at the Inches.* The Inches here has its Scots meaning – a stretch of low lying land near a river. This area disappeared when Commercial Quay was constructed. This scene from the 1880's shows herring being packed into barrels of salt for export. Herring fishing was eclipsed in commercial importance by the growth of the white fish trade from about this time.

46. *Paddle tug.* The great sailing fleets of the 19th century were only made possible by steam paddle tugs. This particular tug is probably the wooden-hulled 'Granite City'. She is shown assisting a small steamer out of the Harbour but she could be essential to the square riggers and schooners whose masts loom above the fishing vessel to the right. Paddle vessels may look quaint but one should not underestimate their sea-going qualities. In the 1970's a redundant paddle tug steamed from Newcastle-on-Tyne across the Atlantic to a museum in California.

47. *Tugs.* The tugs 'St. Machar' and 'St. Fotin' are moored at Pocra Quay with the collier 'Redhall' behind them. In the distance is 'St. Sunniva', the second ship of that name which was built in 1931 by Hall Russell. A 1,368 ton vessel with anachronistic yacht-like lines, she sank on Russian convoy duties in 1943. Her upperworks became encrusted in ice, she turned turtle and sank with all hands. The collier survived two world wars and was finally scrapped in 1959.

48. *Sunlit waters.* The great days of sail were over by the time this view was taken, the warship squadron suggests The Great War. In the 1850's and 1860's Aberdeen led the world in the design and development of fast sailing ships, including many clippers for the China trade. Contemporary accounts do not call them 'tea' clippers. The vessel in this photograph is a ship that is square rigged on all three masts but she is not a clipper. She is one of the later iron or steel hulled ships with a rather slab-sided appearance. Although not as beautiful as a clipper her greater cargo carrying capacity made such craft financially viable long after the true clippers disappeared. The names of several Aberdeen built clippers carry a familiar ring including 'Bon-Accord', 'Abergeldie', 'Cairngorm' and 'City of Aberdeen'.

49. *Aberdeen from Balnagask*. The steam trawlers passing one another are 'Loch Awe'. A.274 and the 'Ocean Princess' A.580. The former was built by Hall Russell in 1909 and was owned by the Loch Line Steam Trawl & Fishing Company in the 1920's. The 'Ocean Princess' belonged to the Aberdeen Fish Supply Association and was built in Glasgow in 1902. The card shows tugs moored behind the jetty and a fair sized ship in the floating dock. From its size and location it is fairly safe to assume that it is Dock No. 3 which was in service from 1911 until 1960. The dock was 310 feet long and could lift 5,000 ton vessels. The oil rush has led to many changes in this scene including the construction of oil tanks and a large covered slipway on the right.

50. *Riverside Road, 'Torry'.* An incorrectly identified card shows the foot of Wellington Bridge looking towards the city centre. The Queen Elizabeth Bridge now sweeps across the foreground. Edwardian cards usually call this a 'road' not a 'drive'. This channel was dug by navvies between 1869 and 1872 diverting the River Don from Wellington Bridge to the tidal harbour.

51. *Westburn Road.* An attractive hand-tinted card posted on 27 April 1911. Its most obvious feature is the spelling mistake in 'Westbourne'. It shows typical solid Aberdeen town houses. It is curious that with the Westburn Park opposite so many children chose to play on the road. The message on the card reads: 'Surely the exertion of the spring cleaning has been too much for your arms and hands when they can't even hold a hen', and reminds us that before the days of convenience foods and oven-ready chickens a high proportion of householders kept hens for both eggs and the table.

52. *Great Western Road.* This card was published by James Donald, 395 Union Street, and was posted from 310 Great Western Road. The message reads: 'I am staying here for a few days with my brother (The Rev) and his wife. I have marked his house. These streets are all a very light coloured granite and look nice among the green trees. There is a private bowling green and lawn tennis grounds immediately opposite. A.P.' The postmark is unclear but 'Buy War Bonds' places it between 1914-1918. Little has changed since this description.

53. *Queen's Cross.* Queen's Cross Church was built as a Free Church in 1881 to a very attractive and individual design by J.B. Pirie. At that time the western part of the City was expanding rapidly and this large church was a sign of the area's prosperity. The large lamp post has been replaced by a statue of Queen Victoria, originally in St. Nicholas Street.

54. *Fountainhall Road.* Fountainhall Road was laid out in the 1880's and as late as 1915 a guidebook said that this was the outskirts of the City with the countryside in sight. Rubislaw Church was built in 1875 as the Established Church recovered from the Disruption. It is unusual in Aberdeen in that it is built of sandstone, the tower being a later addition in response to the splendid spire of the Free Church on the other side of the crossroads. In the distance are two trams, one with an open top and the other closed, which dates the view to about 1910.

55. *Rubislaw Den South.* Rubislaw Den South is a road of handsome properties mainly built at the turn of the century. The nearest house is one of a pair designed by Arthur Clyne, with a mixture of white and pink granite.

Queen's Road, Aberdeen.

56. *Queen's Road.* Rubislaw Supply Stores occupied a building which is still a shop. This is one of Aberdeen's oldest buildings having been built as a toll house. This has always been an area 'where the gentry bide'. The card dates from about 1910 when residents included solicitors and advocates, a Fleet Surgeon, County Chief Constable, Chief Inspector of Schools, a stockbroker and Sir Alexander Lyon (see card 139).

57. *Hamilton Place.* Hamilton Place contains some of Aberdeen's finest residential property with a variety of impressive semi-detached houses. The road is named after Dr. Hamilton who was a Professor of Mathematics at Marischal College and did useful work on the City's water supply. In 1912 it was not quite as 'posh' as Queen's Road as residents included a dressmaker, a cashier, a baker and a plumber among the solicitors and dentists!

ROSEMOUNT PLACE FROM WATSON STREET, ABERDEEN.

58. *Rosemount Place.* The corner of Watson Street with Rosemount Place is shown on this card posted in June 1914. This area, a mixture of houses and tenements, largely dates from the 1870's. The sender marked where she was living at 185 Rosemount Place. A newspaper headline proclaims 'Miners congress denounces jingoism' which suggests early 1914.

59. *United Free Church College.* The College was built in 1850 to train Free Church Ministers. The Disruption and foundation of the Free Church of Scotland had taken place in 1843 over the question of patronage. The Free Church of Scotland united with the United Presbyterian Church to form the United Free Church in 1900. This corner is known as 'Babbie Law's' from its association with the grocery and spirits shop that used to have a considerable reputation in the locality.

60. *Coronation procession.* King George V reigned from 1910 to 1936, most of the period covered by this book. A Coronation Procession was organised in Aberdeen on 11 June 1911. In this view part of the pageant is in King Street, just past Jasmine Terrace. Photographs of King George and Queen Mary can be seen in the windows of a branch of the Northern Co-operative Society.

61. *Guild Street.* Guild Street is named after Dr. William Guild, the Principal of King's College who donated Trinity Hall to the Seven Incorporated Trades in 1663. On the left-hand side of the road can be seen Her Majesty's Theatre built in 1872. It closed between 1906 and 1910, reopened as the Tivoli with a variety programme and became a bingo hall in the 1960's. On the right are the entrances to the Caledonian Railway and the North British Railway goods depots. The Joint Station is behind.

62. *Market Street.* Prominent on the right hand side of the street is the Douglas Hotel. Originally it was the North of Scotland Coffee House. Thomas Douglas purchased it and changed the name in 1849, developing the premises into one of the city's finest hotels. The card dates from early in the century. It was run by, in turn, Andrew Stott and his widow between 1884 and 1919. After a number of changes of ownership, and for a while its name, the Douglas was refurbished in 1989. The Waverley Hotel stood at the bottom of the street opposite the Post Office.

63. *Guest Row.* For the first half of the century this building was known as Cumberland House. It had been occupied by 'Butcher' Cumberland for six weeks in 1746 before Culloden. He helped himself to other people's property during this occupation, adding to his unsavoury reputation. It was restored in 1951 and is now more properly called Provost Skene's House. The Provost considerably extended an older building about 1670. It is a domestic museum with many original features including oak panelling from the eighteenth century, earlier paintings and a number of attractive plaster ceilings. All the surrounding buildings have been demolished in the name of progress leaving this the only survivor of the entire street. Guest Row may be a corruption of Ghostrow as it ran alongside the graveyard!

The Duke of Cumberland's House, 45 Guest Row, Aberdeen.
Built in 1669 by Sir George Skene and occupied for 6 weeks by the Duke of Cumberland in 1746.

64. *Salmon fishers.* Salmon fishing rights were granted to the Burgh of Aberdeen by Robert the Bruce. In the middle ages salmon became Aberdeen's first major export. By the 1700's thousands of barrels were shipped to London alone. Fishing seasons and methods have always been carefully regulated in order to conserve stock, including a ban on the use of nets at weekends. Cobles were rowed in a circle on the river and then the nets were pulled to the shore where additional fishermen helped to land the catch. Fixed nets were only permitted on the sea beaches, not in the rivers. Salmon stocks have reduced in recent years despite the additional stock released from the Dee Hatchery at Dinnet. The Harbour Board continues to regulate salmon fishing on behalf of the City maintaining a 650 year practice.

CONSOLE OF ORGAN BUILT BY E. H. LAWTON, PITTODRIE ORGAN WORKS, ABERDEEN

65. *Pittodrie Organ Works*. In 1866 the Church of Scotland permitted the installation of organs for services and a boom in organ construction followed. E.H. Lawton, located at Ardarroch Road and Linksfield Road, supplied organs to many of the city's places of worship. A list compiled in 1966 showed a dozen of their instruments including Powis Church (1909), John Knox, Mounthooley (1903), Crown Terrace Baptist Church (1937), St. Peter's Roman Catholic Church (1927), Trinity Congregational Church (1904) and the Grammar School (1930). This company was obviously prepared to work for any denomination!

66. *Tailors.* The City's own regiment, the Gordon Highlanders, are shown tailoring kilts. The Castlehill barracks were in use from the 1790's until 1935 when new barracks were built along Ellon Road. The original barracks were demolished in 1965 and the site is now occupied by Virginia and Marischal Courts. The Regiment has a fine history including battle honours in the Boer War and was made an Honorary Burgess of the City in 1956.

Aberdeen Military Training Association, or City Guard.

67. *Aberdeen Military Training Association.* The Aberdeen Military Training Association was formed in November 1914 to encourage recruiting to the armed forces, to render such voluntary service to the Country as its Committee considered advisable and to provide military training to men in Aberdeen who were unable or ineligible to join the Regular Army or Territorials. The Chairman was Lord Provost James Taggart. The Committee set a minimum subscription of one shilling and provided training in drill and shooting. The application form deliberately asked detailed questions to sort out potential soldiers who were then encouraged to join the Forces. The building in the background appears to be Mannofield Church, which places this drill on the Cricket Ground.

68. *Red Cross transport waggons.* The Red Cross movement was established in 1863 to protect the wounded, the personnel caring for them and medical supplies for their use. Later Red Cross activities were extended to cover victims of war at sea, prisoners of war and civilians during wars. During the First World War the Scottish Branch of the Red Cross provided nurses, hospitals and ambulances wherever British Forces were engaged. Scotland furnished 629 ambulances of which 134 were gifts including these two provided by Scottish Bowlers and the Licensed Trades which were used in Aberdeen during 1916 and 1917. Scottish ambulances served on all fronts including Russia and France. In Aberdeen the Transport Service carried 253,000 patients during the war under the supervision of Mr. Bennett Mitchell, M.B.E. Today the Red Cross, together with the Red Crescent in Muslim countries, operates in 147 countries and has expanded into new areas of work as varied as cosmetic camouflage advice and international tracing.

69. *Mansefield Dairy.* Victoria Road, Torry, still has the shop which was this dairy but it is presently used as a decorator's store room. The lady on the card is presumably Annie Lindsay who, in a message on the card, recalls having the picture taken the previous year.

70. *House of Sweets.* This card shows part of the interior of John Esslemont's shop at 16-22 King Street which surely does justice to the Aberdonian's sweet tooth. Mr. Esslemont also ran King Street Post Office and a family grocers. The name of John E. Esslemont still remains painted across these buildings in King Street although the premises are now occupied by a variety of businesses. On the reverse of this card John E. Esslemont advertises a special exhibition of 'confectionery, tea, provisions, groceries, bakers' sundries and chemists' specialities' for Highland Show Week.

71. *Dentist's house in King Street.* A little way down King Street from the House of Sweets! This card appears to date from the 1920's and shows 173 King Street as a dental surgery occupied by Mr. A.R. Grosert, one of the three dentists in the street.

72. *Smoking haddies.* The curing or smoking of haddock by various local methods was the backbone of the winter fishing season in the nineteenth century. It initially arose in north-east villages such as Findon, a few miles south of Aberdeen, home of the 'Finnan Haddie'. Originally a cottage industry, the arrival of the railways created an opportunity for a large scale industry to develop. A steady demand from Glasgow provided a market and by 1900 Aberdeen had 100 curing businesses. A few are shown here.

73. *La Scala Tea Rooms.* In 1700 a George Cruickshank set up an establishment to sell coffee, tea and chocolate and such businesses have been popular ever since. The La Scala Cinema opened in 1914 at 234 Union Street. The Tea Rooms were run as a separate enterprise in accommodation decorated in a so-called Chinese style using a black, green, gold and pink colour scheme. It proved so successful that it extended into a neighbouring building shortly after it opened. It is alleged that during the war the Tea Rooms were particularly popular with members of the forces hoping to meet ladies of easy virtue. By the 1920's patrons were attracted by the more seemly virtues of a violinist and a pianist. 'Talkies' arrived in the late twenties but the cinema closed in 1935 so that the Majestic Cinema could be developed on this site.

74. *Stoneywood Mill.* Stoneywood Mill is a very self sufficient enterprise. In 1894 it had its own gas works, waterwheels and used tons of coal. Every 24 hours it produced 150 miles of paper to a six or seven foot width – and some people think Henry Ford invented mass production! Two of the chimneys were over 200 feet high.

75. *Stoneywood House.* Built in the Jacobean style circa 1849 for the paper manufacturer Alexander Pirie, the house stands close to the Mill. It is currently used as a training centre by the paper mill. The card was published by John Gray, Bucksburn and posted in 1907.

76. *Rubislaw Quarry*. Rubislaw Quarry appears on this card posted in 1906. Rubislaw was surveyed with granite quarrying in mind as early as 1740. However, as is well known errors delayed production until John Gibb took a lease some years later. During its working life the quarry produced about 6 million tons of granite before closing in 1971. The 480 feet deep and 900 feet long hole remains a conspicuous suburban landmark.

77. *Granite yard.* Granite use in Aberdeen dates back to the middle ages when stones were gathered from open ground for building purposes, St. Machar's being the prime example. Later the use of granite setts as paving stones became so popular that by 1790 over 600 men were employed in the business. Dressed granite came into use for civil engineering from early in the nineteenth century. By 1914 there were 90 odd yards ranging in size from a handful of men to enterprises with over 100 employees. This card illustrates one of the larger yards with an overhead crane for moving the blocks of stone.

78. *Granite cross.* In 1830 Alexander MacDonald devised the first mechanical means of cutting and polishing granite. An iron bladed saw swung to and fro across the rock using an abrasive which was originally seaside sand. Polishing was achieved by moving granite blocks on bogies over fixed iron rings, again using sharp sand as an abrasive. The card shows pneumatic chisels in use at the turn of the century. Compressed air was also used to power hammers and drills. The men are finishing a Celtic cross but could easily have been preparing cladding for an office, carving memorials or shaping rollers for industrial uses. The pneumatic tools were probably made by the Bon Accord Tool Co., St. Clair Street, Aberdeen.

79. *Royal Infirmary*. The first Infirmary was built at Woolmanhill in 1741. The Royal Infirmary was built in 1822 and expanded to 240 beds during Queen Victoria's Jubilee Year of 1887. In 1907 the hospital treated without charge those unable to pay except those on parochial aid who required a recommendation from the Inspector of Poor of the Parish to which they belonged. The Infirmary averaged 218 patients in their care and during the course of that year the Hospital spent £11,763 from an income of £11,978 – a far cry from today.

80. *Old Mill Hospital.* Now known as Woodend Hospital, the Old Mill Hospital was opened on 15 May 1907. The total cost of the structure, including the purchase of the estate of Old Mill, was £130,000. During the Great War, Old Mill was evacuated and used entirely as a military hospital and was reopened as Woodend Hospital in October 1927. There appears to be a concert by a military band on this card posted in 1918.

81. *New Infirmary, Foresterhill.* Aberdeen has a long history in medical science. King's College had 'Mediciners' from 1522 and Marischal College has had a Professor of Medicine since 1700. The New Infirmary was opened in 1936 by the Duke and Duchess of York, later to become King George VI and Queen Elizabeth. Needless to say it was paid for by public subscription. Additions over the last fifty years have altered this view considerably.

82. *Central School.* The Central Public School opened in 1894 as a centre for senior pupils from the free schools in the City. The school prospered and developed a reputation for educating future pupil teachers. A new main building on the corner of Belmont Street and Schoolhill was built and occupied in 1905 as the Central Higher Grade School. The School was evacuated from 1914 to 1919 and from 1939 to 1944 but remained on this site until 1970. In 1954 the School changed its name to Aberdeen Academy. The introduction of comprehensive education led to a new name, Hazlehead Academy, and a new location in Hazlehead. The old school building is now a Resources Centre for the Education Authority. The School had remarkable stability in its headmasters, Mr. A.G. Wallace served from 1894-1926 followed by Mr. J.W. Robertson to 1954 when Mr. Alexander Goldie arrived. Former pupils include opera singers, actors, sportsmen and a Member of Parliament.

83. *Gordon's College.* The 'tin palaces' were in place in the forecourt of Gordon's College between 1911 and 1931. In 1911 the East Wing was gutted by fire and to provide temporary accommodation the College built wooden structures on brick foundations with corrugated iron roofs. There were 12 classrooms and a physics laboratory. This scene is much changed with lawns replacing these 'tin palaces' and several new blocks which compliment the original Auld Hoose shown in the centre of the photograph. Today the site is shared by Robert Gordon's College and Robert Gordon's Institute of Technology.

Girls' High School, Albyn Place, Aberdeen.

84. *High School for Girls.* Archibald Simpson designed several buildings in Albyn Place in the 1830's including this one for orphan girls. Mrs. Elmslie's Institute or Girl's Academy, founded in 1874, became the High School for Girls in 1881. It moved into this building in 1893 and was renamed the Harlaw Academy in 1970. It became a six year comprehensive school which has since become co-educational. The school has educated many professional people but perhaps the best known 'old girls' are in the entertainment world, particularly the cookery expert Katie Stewart and pop-singer Annie Lennox.

85. *St. Mary's School.* There was a St. Mary's Roman Catholic primary school in Summer Street immediately before and after the First World War. This card has printed on it 'St. Mary's School' and 8 Beaconsfield Place has been hand written on top. This is presumably an annex to the school. Patrick McGrath was the teacher. This substantial property was designed by James Souttar, the same architect who designed the Salvation Army Citadel.

86. *Grammar School.* An Act of 1496, sponsored by Aberdeen's Bishop Elphinstone, directed that the sons of Barons and Freeholders were to be put to school at 8 or 9 years of age. This was not implemented but schools grew anyway. The Grammar School descends from the medieval Burgh school and has been located in this Scottish baronial style building since 1863. The School dropped its fee paying basis in 1944 but did not admit girls until 1973. It burnt out in July 1986 and at the time of writing the plans to rebuild have not come to fruition. The architect, Archibald Simpson (1790-1847), was educated at the Grammar School. The fruits of his practice, established in Aberdeen in 1813, remain some of the City's finest buildings.

87. *Byron's statue.* Lord George Byron, the Grammar School's most notorious pupil, began his education in Aberdeen before Harrow and Cambridge. His Aberdeen childhood contains many clues to his later life. He was 'in love' for the first of many occasions at the age of eight to his cousin, Mary Duff. It is said that 'to his Scottish upbringing he owed his love and knowledge of the Bible and too much Calvinism for faith or unfaith in Christianity'. The Grammar School, which was on Schoolhill when he was a pupil, erected the statue in 1923.

88. *Aberdeen Art Gallery.* The absence of trees in front of the gallery suggests the turn of the century. This photograph of the Art Gallery was taken from the roof of the building across the road. On this G.W. Wilson card, Gordon's College can be seen over the central gateway. The Gallery houses one of Scotland's finest art collections. It is particularly strong on Aberdeen artists but also has international stars including Monet, Sisley and Degas. The statue of General Gordon was erected in 1888 by the Clan Gordon following his death in Khartoum three years earlier. It is fashionable to mock the empire building activities of such men but we should remember that Gordon was partly motivated by a wish to stamp out the slave trade.

89. *Art Gallery Interior.* The Sculpture Court was erected by public subscription in 1885. The Gallery displayed several examples of Scottish stoneworking skills – in this card they appear to be of a religious nature. In 1902 it was joined by a gallery displaying plaster casts of Roman, Greek, French and Italian sculpture. The idea had come from a local grain merchant, Dr. John Forbes White. In the late 1960's much of this material was placed in store but recently some items have been returned. Note the radiators – museum pieces in their own right!

90. *General Post Office.* The General Post Office, built in Crown Street in 1906, is yet another building influenced by Balmoral Castle. In 1915 it was open from 6.45 am to 10.00 pm, Monday to Saturday and between 9.00 – 10.00 am and 1.00 2.00 pm on Sundays! It appears that the steps in the centre of the picture originally led to a solid wall. The advertisement shows that 'My Mimosa Maid' was the current production at His Majesty's Theatre. No doubt, with snow on the ground, Bovril was a welcome drink even if it did not 'repel influenza' as claimed on the hoarding. The Post Office recently moved from this site to premises in Union Street.

91. *Post Office interior.* This card shows the Instrument Room in the newly opened Post Office, according to its sender. Unfortunately, it is not clear which instruments are referred to, it may be telegraphy as no telephone switchgear is in sight. The first recorded suggestion for an electric telegraph was made in Scotland by an anonymous writer to Scots Magazine in 1753. The writer suggested a separate wire for each letter of the alphabet.

92. *Bridge Of Dee from farm.* From a pre-World War I series, this card shows the view from South Deeside Road with the bridge in the distance. The horse-drawn plough in the foreground would have been a common sight for a further 30 years as tractors only outnumbered farm horses as recently as 1948. The first combine harvester appeared in Scotland in 1932. It has been said that 'scratch an Aberdonian and you will find a countryman' and this card reminds us that the City is as dependent on agriculture as it is on the more commonly depicted fishing industry and granite quarrying.

93. *Bridge Of Dee close up*. Two hundred years younger than the Brig o'Balgownie, the Bridge of Dee is still one of the oldest Scottish bridges. It was completed in the 1520's and has been rebuilt and widened since. It has been the site of two battles and it is reported that cannon balls from 1639 still occasionally turn up at Kaimhill! The large white building is Ruthrieston School.

94. *Brig O'Balgownie.* The ancient Brig o'Balgownie was built by a Provost of Aberdeen, Richard Cementarius in 1318 and has been repaired and modified on several occasions since. For six hundred years it was the only crossing of the Don near the City. It is frequently depicted on postcards but they neither capture the picturesqueness of the spot nor the size of the arch as it vaults the river. In this view a fisherman spreads a net. Sir Alexander Hay established a fund to repair the bridge in 1603 which eventually provided the capital to construct the Bridge of Don downstream.

95. *Bridge of Don.* The Bridge of Don was built in 1827 and the widening of 1958 carefully duplicated the original stonework. The Don View Bar has a lot more neighbours today. The quality of the water varies considerably at this point; at its best this is a good bird spotting site. However the 'Don Pong' can occasionally strike, caused by polluted water.

96. *Grandholm Bridge.* Grandholm Bridge, reflected in the Don, leads to Grandholm Mill. The Mill dates back to 1792. It has housed Crombie's Woollen Mill since the death of their founder John Crombie in 1858. This idyllic corner, only three miles from the City centre, is deceptive in that only just a few yards upstream there are remains of several industrial sites.

97. *Suspension Bridge.* Until the Victoria Bridge was built in 1881, the Wellington Suspension Bridge was the only alternative crossing to the Bridge of Dee. The bridge dates from 1829-31. Originally the frame and rods were made of iron but the wooden deck is now steel framed. Flat link chains support the bridge which results in its nickname the 'chain briggie'.

98. *Hazlehead Park*. The original Tea Rooms in Hazlehead Park, shown here in the 1920's, have been replaced by a modern structure. Hazlehead Park was purchased from the Rose family in 1920. Its 680 acres are dominated by one 9 hole and two 18 hole golf courses. The park also has football pitches and other sporting facilities. There are over 100 acres of woodland, acres of azaleas and heathers. Clydesdale horses have been working in the grounds since 1980 when they became more economic than vans for this type of work.

99. *Duthie Park*. Duthie Park was given to the City by Miss Charlotte Duthie of Ruthrieston and opened by Queen Victoria's daughter, Princess Beatrice, in 1883. The Winter Gardens seen today were built in 1972 to replace the beautiful structure of 1890-1900 which was demolished after gale damage in 1969. The gatehouse shown in this card was dismantled because of road widening in 1937 and now stands as No 72 Rubislaw Den South. The Peterhead granite obelisk, which appears outside Marischal College on another card, was moved to the park in 1906. It is a memorial to Sir James McGrigor, the founder of the Army Medical Corps. Duthie Park, with a variety of features in its 44 acres, may be the City's most attractive open space.

100. *Westburn Park*. Westburn Park was established in 1901 by Aberdeen Town Council. The Westburn stream has been widened into children's paddling pools. This park has developed as an active recreation centre and was the scene of a recent World Bowls Championships.

101. *Victoria Park.* Victoria Park is the city's oldest surviving park dating from 1871. It originally comprised four fields covering fourteen acres. It is a tranquil park and includes a garden for the blind with highly scented flowers and others to touch with labels in Braille. The fountain, constructed from fourteen different granites, is floodlit in summer. The Parks Department was established in 1878 to maintain the area.

102. *Persley Den.* Persley Den is largely surrounded by built-up areas but boasts an impressive range of wildlife. The authors disturbed a roe deer recently and buzzards and heron are regular visitors. The Nature Trail between Grandholm and Persley Bridges passes a wide variety of trees including oak, ash, holly, elm and beech.

103. *Shakkin' Briggie.* The 'Shakkin' Briggie' was built to serve the church at Nether Banchory. It is more properly named St. Devenick's Bridge. Dr. George Morrison, the Minister of Elsick, erected it in 1837. It was closed in 1958 after the foundations were damaged by serious floods. It had been insecure for many years, hence its nickname. The foundations have partly impeded the flow of the river at this point which has to some extent preserved gravel beds on which can be found Arctic and Alpine flowers.

104. *Paper Mill, Culter.* This paper mill opened in 1751, having been set up by Bartholomew Smith, an Englishman. For many years it was the only industrial activity in Peterculter. They specialised in fine writing papers including, for a while, a unique paper differently tinted on each side. As recently as the 1970's over 600 people were employed here but it closed in 1980. A housing estate now occupies the site.

105. *United Free Church, Newhills.* Rev. Thomas B. Robertson was Minister of the United Free Church, Newhills, between 1911 and 1917. He was born in India in 1882 and educated at Aberdeen Grammar School. He studied Divinity at Aberdeen, becoming Minister in 1908 at Kingswell Church. He married Grace Simpson the following year. It is believed that he had two children. He died aged only 44, while he was Minister in St. Cyrus. The Church, completed in 1844 as the Free Church of Newhills, is today Bucksburn Church of Scotland. It says much for the idealism, energy and hard work of the community that the Church was dedicated only a year after the Disruption.

106. *Woodside Fountain.* Woodside Fountain was located at the heart of Woodside where Western Road crosses Great Northern Road. Woodside has been settled since at least the fifteenth century, growing rapidly in the nineteenth century. It was an independent Burgh from 1868 to 1891, when it was absorbed into the City. J. & T. Fisher's grocery shop on the corner appears to display bathtubs and other hardware. We can also see a horse drinking from the fountain. Aberdeen's first electric tramcar No. 1 passes towards Bankhead. The final tramcar to Woodside ran in 1955, three years before all trams in the City were withdrawn from service.

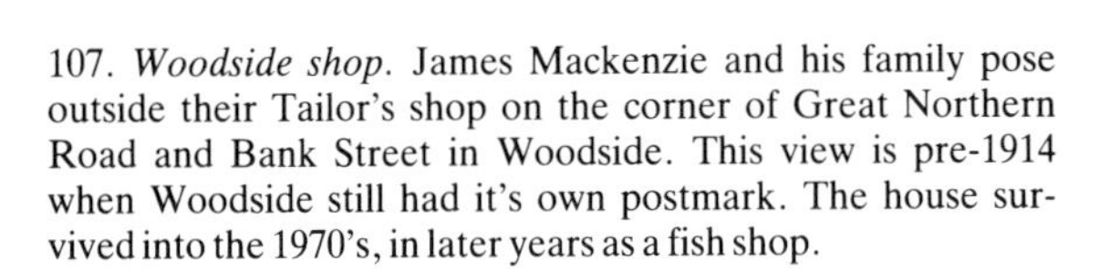
107. *Woodside shop.* James Mackenzie and his family pose outside their Tailor's shop on the corner of Great Northern Road and Bank Street in Woodside. This view is pre-1914 when Woodside still had it's own postmark. The house survived into the 1970's, in later years as a fish shop.

108. *St. Joseph's Church, Woodside.* The Catholic Emancipation Act 1829 did not lead to an immediate expansion of the Roman Catholic Church in Scotland. This chapel, the second R.C. Church in Aberdeen, dates from 1842. A later landmark was the 1875 publication in Aberdeen of the New Testament translated into Scots Gaelic. An episcopal hierarchy was set up in 1878. This interior was altered following the second Vatican Council in the 1960's.

109. *Shetland ponies at Dyce.* Arable crops and raising beef cattle were not the only farming activities around Aberdeen. On this card Mr. Thomas Skinner of Newton Farm, Dyce, wrote to a London address in 1909. He said that he had just sold a pony to a gentleman in Sussex and offers for sale a jet black pedigree 'horse' 36 inches high and two years old. He does not give a price.

110. *Blairs College.* Blairs was originally an estate owned by the Menzies family of Pitfodels, who gave it to the Roman Catholic Church in 1827 to use as a seminary. These buildings were erected between 1897 and 1901. The College was closed in the 1980's.

111. *Blairs College, Library.* Blairs College library, shown in this 1934 card, had a fine collection of illustrated manuscripts and over 150 early printed books. Other items of interest included portraits of Mary Queen of Scots and the Blair papers which had been smuggled out of the Scots College in Paris during the French Revolution. The books have since been transferred to the National Library in Edinburgh.

112. *Balmedie Eventide Home.* In 1937 Balmedie House was a mansion in extensive grounds with no gas or electricity and limited accommodation. However, it was purchased from the Dept. of Agriculture and altered and fitted out by the Church of Scotland as an Eventide Home. It provides accommodation for 40 elderly people. It opened on 27 October 1937 with a Miss Mackintosh as the first Matron. She was succeeded in 1939 by Mr. and Mrs. W.E. Parrott who remained for twenty years.

113. *Balmedie, interior view.* A pre-war card shows the interior of the Eventide Home. In 1962 a number of changes were made to the Home including the renewal of the furniture. During its first 25 years perhaps the most colourful resident was Mrs. Helen Campbell, an actress and playwright. In 1954 she was interviewed for 'Everybody's' magazine and dealt with the question of being too old at forty. She said 'At Balmedie Eventide Home all the outside work is done by men over eighty – hoeing, sowing, digging and planting. One man of 86 is an expert scythe man, another of 84 carries letters and parcels and in his spare time rakes the walks... I myself am 80 and still writing for the B.B.C... Too old at eighty? Fiddlesticks.'

114. *Golf at Balnagask.* Golf has been played in Aberdeen since 1538 and on Queens Links since at least 1625. In 1875 there were only 28 courses in Scotland but between 1891 and 1910 half of today's 430 courses were built. By 1914 there were five courses in the City and visitors to Balnagask paid one shilling (5p) a round or one shilling and sixpence a day. This was expensive compared with the Municipal course at the beach which was only two old pence per round. Royal Aberdeen Golf Club is the sixth oldest in the world. It was reformed in 1815 as the successor to the Society of Aberdeen Golfers founded in 1780. The club moved from the Links in 1888 because of various disturbances, including turf cutting to repair the race course. The Club's great contribution to the game was to introduce a rule in 1783 permitting only five minutes to find a missing ball.

A South-Easter at the Breakwater, Aberdeen

115. *Breakwater*. This is an advertising card for G.W. Wilson & Co., 2 St. Swithin Street. They offer Collotype pictorial postcards in black, sepia or green/black.

250 of a subject....................................	10s 6d
500 of a subject....................................	18s 6d
1000 of a subject....................................	25 shillings (£1.25p)

Postage was one half penny (½d) and postcards were sold by the million.

116. *Girdleness Lighthouse.* Girdleness Lighthouse, built in 1833, stands 120 feet high and the climb to the top is 189 steps. The double flash every twenty seconds is visible for 19 miles. The Girdle in question is an offshore rock. Girdleness gave its name to a Royal Naval guided missile trials ship, a strange contrast with the lifesaving duties of the old light. In the distance can be seen over thirty sailing craft.

117. *Bay of Nigg.* The Bay of Nigg, a popular beach in the years between the wars, offered tea rooms, ice creams and swings to day trippers. In 1805 the last duel fought with pistols in Aberdeen took place here. It is now the base for competing oil company headquarters.

118. *Victoria Road, Torry.* Torry had been settled by fisher folk for hundreds of years when the Victoria Bridge opened in 1881. Victoria Road was built two years later and is typical of the solid tenements of the time. The card shows tramcar No. 43 in its open top days. The same vehicle can be seen in Union Street on Card 28 after a roof had been added. This area was badly damaged in an air-raid in July 1941 when Victoria Road School was destroyed.

119. *Torry bus.* A mid 1920's card shows one of the first private buses in Aberdeen. It ran from one end of the City to the other, from Woodside to Torry. It is clear that, in common with many vehicles at this time, it has no brakes on the front wheels. The notice in the background reads 'Balnagask Golf Club – Cars MUST be parked here'.

120. *Bowling Green.* The beach in the late 1920's showing the Beach Ballroom, Bowling Greens and Lawn Tennis Courts. Eight trams are in view compared with only three motor cars. Harry Gordon, the comedian, was playing to packed houses at the Beach Pavilion at this period.

121. *Beach and Bathing Station.* The beach on a card posted in January 1917 is crowded with people. Points of interest include an early slot machine, the individually numbered bathing coaches on wheels, the fishing nets just beyond the breakers and well covered up beachgoers!

122. *Bathing Station.* The beach on a card posted in 1912. Beyond the Bathing Station were an Amusement Pavilion, Zoo, Skating Rink and Battery. These buildings backed onto the Queen's Links, which was the site of a Race Course.

123. *Pierrots.* Fred Parr's Pierrots were an early attraction on the beach but we have been unable to identify this particular troop.

124. *The Bathing Station.* The landward side of The Aberdeen Corporation's Bathing Station is shown about 1907. It advertised a Russo-Turkish bath, first and second class private baths with hot or cold water and sea water. The swimming pool used sea water heated to 74°F. Medicated baths and refreshments were also provided. The popularity of the beach increased considerably with the introduction of the electric tram service.

125. *Scenic Railway.* The Scenic Railway was a switchback railway built by American John Henry Iles. It was a dominant feature of the amusement park in the 1930's. It was extensively damaged in a fire in December 1940 and the charred remains were scrapped.

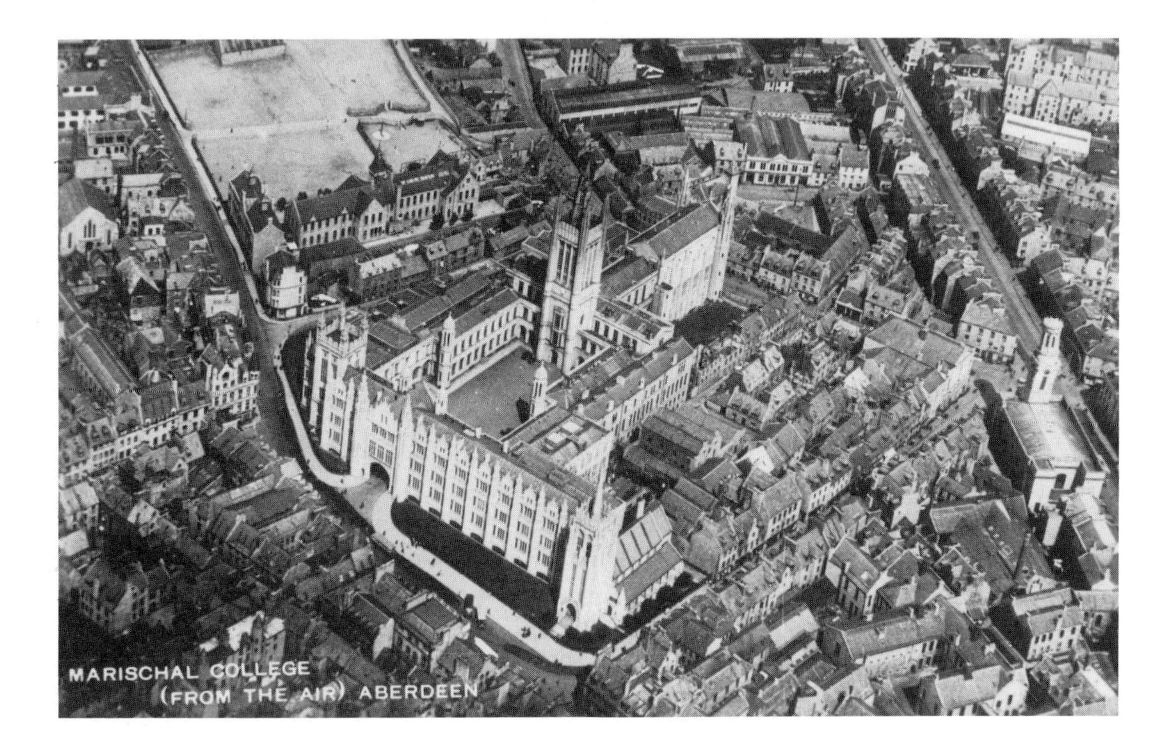

126. *Marischal College aerial View.* This view from before 1937 shows the complete complex of Marischal College which comprises the world's second largest granite structure. The eighteenth century buildings lining Queen Street, which run past the right hand side of the College, have since been demolished and St. Katherine's Shopping Centre built on North Street. The North Church on the right of the card survives as Aberdeen Arts Centre.

127. *Marischal College.* Marischal College was established in 1593 by George Keith, fifth Earl Marischal, on land which was originally occupied by a monastery. The central block which dates from 1840 is overshadowed by the 260 feet high Mitchell Tower. The College amalgamated with King's College in 1860.

128. *Old Greyfriars.* The old Greyfriars Church stood in the way of the development of Marischal College and in 1906 it was demolished. On this site now stands the familiar frontage of the College opened in 1906. The South window was saved and built into the new Greyfriars Church at the east end. The old church was erected in 1518-32 by a reformed order of Greyfriars, the observantine Franciscans. The obelisk shown on this card was moved to Duthie Park where it still stands.

129. *New Greyfriars Church.* This card, although not postally used, can be closely dated. It shows the church shortly after it replaced the earlier church illustrated elsewhere but before the Broad Street frontage of Marischal College was built. Therefore, it shows the position in 1904-5. The obelisk is still in place and work is in hand on the foundations on the left. This card has a divided back but has not quite lost the habit of leaving space for a message on the front and was printed in Saxony.

130. *Byron's House.* This card was posted in May 1906 and shows Byron's childhood home. Byron's mother who was from Gight, Aberdeenshire, moved to Aberdeen in 1790 with her baby son. They lived in this three storey house until 1798 when Byron inherited a title from a great uncle. The house was demolished to provide space for the Marischal College extension at the turn of the century. Byron had few illusions about the property – he said 'it was a change from a shabby Scotch flat to a palace'.

131. *Railway locomotive.* Pictured in Aberdeen Railway Station is L.M.S. No. 14450 in the red livery used from 1923 to 1927. She was built for Caledonian Railways in May 1913 as a McIntosh 'Dunalister IV', No. 43. This was the first series of Scottish locomotives fitted with superheaters. A successful class of 4-4-0 machines, this fine engine was scrapped in 1955 by which time she was serving a third company, British Railways. Points of interest include a single Pullman carriage and a very crowded signal gantry. The scene is strangely peaceful after the notorious rail races of the late nineteenth century when, in order to set a record between London and Aberdeen, trains ran with only three coaches covering 540 miles in 512 minutes.

132. *S.S. 'St. Clair'*. 'St. Clair' is a name which has been carried by a series of vessels on the Aberdeen to Shetland run. The earlier ships were operated by the North of Scotland, Orkney and Shetland Steamship Co. and the more recent ships by P. & O. This particular 'St. Clair' ran from 1937 to 1967 carrying passengers, mail and general cargo. She was the last steam ship in this service. Her replacement had the distinction of being the last two class ship under the Red Ensign. The authors remember Second Class was rather basic for the overnight trip to Lerwick. It was as recently as 1977 that the current 'St. Clair' introduced the roll-on roll-off system to the service.

133. *S.S. 'Aberdonian'*. The Aberdeen Steam Ship Company's 'Aberdonian' sailed from Aberdeen for London. She, together with 'Hogath' and 'City of London', provided a service every Wednesday and Saturday. She had good quality accommodation with a Ladies' Saloon and a Smoking Room. In 1914 the Company's advertisements boasted that she had electric lighting. The 36 hour voyage to London cost one pound and ten shillings for first class passengers and 15 shillings (75p) for second class. The 'Aberdonian' remained in service until the Second World War, having served a spell as a hospital ship in the First World War. When this card was posted in 1928 there was a network of coastal passenger services to the Moray Firth, Leith, Newcastle-on-Tyne and Hull. The last coastal passenger link was the Leith-Aberdeen leg of the Shetland run which continued until the early 1970's.

134. *Horse Bus at Lemon Tree public house.* The Cluny horse-bus was descended from the Vale of Cluny coach. It left Sauchen of Cluny at 7.30 am. for 9 St. Nicholas Street (now occupied by Richards Shops) arriving at 10.00 am. The return trip left at 5.00 pm. The 31 seater bus was usually pulled by four horses but in winter five were used. In the summer they managed with three horses, taking mail to the villages and returning with eggs and butter. The Lemon Tree Bar moved here when Huxter Row was obliterated during the 1880's.

135. *Girls Guildry*. An unposted card, published by Miss Flora Maxwell, 187 Rosemount Viaduct. We assume it shows a Girls Guildry group.

136. *Teachers outing.* A card posted in July 1911 shows some of the 'B teachers at a farewell picnic to Miss Sinclair, who is now Mrs. Forsyth'. It was sent to Canada by 'Alick' from 11 Elmbank Road, Aberdeen. The card shows a lovely collection of Edwardian blouses.

137. *Sailors Mission.* The British Sailors' Society had a Sailors Mission in Mearns Street until 1985 when it closed after over a century of service to the seafaring community. The card was posted in 1909 and probably shows the Sabbath School Choir. In 1908 there were 245 scholars and 22 teachers. The children were drawn almost entirely from sailor families in the district. A Mr. Maitland and Miss Dunn organised the choir and they are presumably the adults in the picture. The Missionary was Mr. Robert C. Seivewright and Mrs. Helen Joss managed the Home. Activities included Bible classes, ship and hospital visits, a Dorcas Society and a savings bank.

138. *N.A.A.F.I. Club.* The Navy, Army and Air Force Institutes, the official trading arm of H.M. Forces operated more than one N.A.A.F.I. Club in Aberdeen. This Club was located at 36/40 Market Street from 11 April 1945 until 11 April 1947 under the management of Mr. C. Turner. The facilities included a Reading Room, Tavern, Dining Room, Cafeteria and Ballroom. Queen Elizabeth and the young Princesses visited the Club before travelling back to London after a Balmoral holiday.

139. *Sir Alexander Lyon.* Sir Alexander Lyon was Lord Provost from 1905 until 1908. The City's motto is based on a tradition, first recorded 150 years after the event, that 'Bon Accord' was the password when the English were expelled from the Castle in 1307. The leopards appeared by 1430, whilst the triple-towered tower of that period has developed into three individual towers today. The red and white colours of Aberdeen Football team are inspired by the silver and red of the Coat of Arms.

140. *Aberdeen on a flag day.* No album of Aberdeen post cards would be complete without a 'Flag Day' card. The first flag day was held in 1915 to benefit sick and wounded horses. Aberdeen has long been a target for jokes about meanness. Aberdonians tend to take such humour as a compliment to the strength of the City's personality, disregarding the slur. Other postcards carry examples of such humour i.e., Overheard in Aberdeen 'The bus conductor glowered at me yesterday as if I hadn't paid my fare. 'What did ye dae?' 'I glowered back at him as if I had'.
Booking clerk at King's Cross to traveller for Inverness 'Change at Aberdeen'.
Traveller, 'Na, na, I'll tak me change noo, I've been tae Aiberdeen afore'.